SMILE

ANYWAYS

Copyright © 2020 Amber Otto
All rights reserved.
ISBN: 978-0-578-71861-3

Dedication

This book is dedicated to not only those who shaped and molded me into the person I am today, but to myself for consistently trying to be strong in the face of adversity. This book is also dedicated to any child or adult who has been in a position of ridicule, judgment or jealously just for simply being different than what society deems as "normal." I hope that in some small way this book can guide you in shining your light because of who you are regardless of the darkness that follows not too far behind.

Contents

1. It all starts with one   pg 5
2. The seed begins to grow   pg 7
3. The waters that nurture   pg 9
4. The seed begins to blossom   pg 11
5. Never forget your roots   pg 13
6. Continued growth   pg 15
7. The soils from which it came   pg 17
8. The best is yet to come   pg 19
9. Don't forget to trim   pg 21
10. Trimming promotes growth   pg 23
11. Growing never stops   pg 24

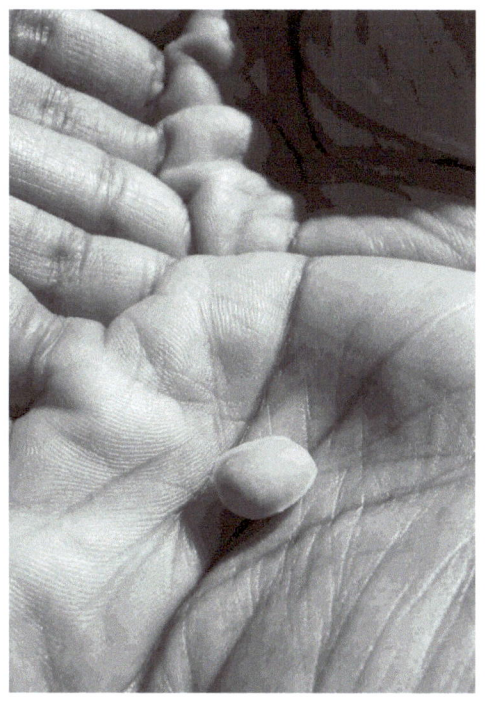

It all starts with one little seed.

———

When the world gets you down all because you're brown, look inside and you will find you have a special light. Every step every mile, is worthwhile when you don't forget to **smile** anyways.

Before you know it, the seed begins to grow

When the world laughs at you and you don't know what to do, do what people don't expect and never forget, to smile anyways.

As it is necessary for the seed to do its job to grow, the waters that nurture it are just as important.

When you feel you want to cry, look up into the sky and know you were made perfect. Every stroke of colored skin, whether you're short or very thin, was no mistake my child and God wants you to smile anyways.

As the seed gradually takes shape, buds of its potential begin to blossom.

In life you will come across people who don't understand you and because they don't, try to hurt your heart. Think Happy thoughts, because your heart is all you've got and in a while you will begin to **smile anyways.**

But it never forgets its roots.

Remember not all people are mean, so don't do unto others as others have done unto you. Even when people are mean, what's going on inside them is not what it seems. Just say a sweet prayer, and hope they get better, so they too can **smile anyways**.

The seed continues to grow and grow and grow…

When the going gets tough and you've had enough, don't be rough and act carelessly. Just know this will pass, because sad feelings never last, when you smile anyways.

And somehow still with all the growth, never forgets the soils in which it began its journey.

Yes you are different but because this is so, you can make a difference in the world. Just show others who you are, like a shimmering star that was meant to stand apart from the very start.

The beautiful thing about a seed is even when it seems as if it's fully bloomed, the best is yet to come…

In getting to know you they will find that you can be kind just like them. They will also see that you can't always be happy because you're human nothing more, nothing less. But even when you're down you can turn that frown upside down and **smile anyways**.

Not only water and sunlight do the trick for the seed, but so it can stand taller and more resilient than before, it needs trimming.

So I hope this message can be your guide to remind you what to do when you're feeling blue and don't want to be you. Be proud of who you are and you will go far as long as you smile anyways.

Trimming helps to not only shape the seed, but give it room for more potential buds to grow.

I hope that the growth and continued transformation of my seed can help you to grow yours. And more importantly I hope that the seeds planted inside your heart can help another's to grow too. Always remember your roots and never let the growing process stop within you. It all depends on you as to how your seed will grow.

www.ingramcontent.com/pod-product-compliance
Lightning Source LLC
Chambersburg PA
CBHW041746040426
42444CB00004B/191